CW01509872

Adhyatma Upanishad

With English Translation and Commentary

Digvijay Shahi

Introduction

The Upanishads are among Hinduism's revered, ancient texts. They offer insights into spirituality, philosophy, and meditation. As a commentary to the Vedas, many sages have contributed to its compilation. They explore the nature of reality, consciousness, and the self through discussions on the universe, the soul, and physics. In summary, the Upanishads are a window to the Veda's knowledge and, hence, the spirit. A person need not study any other philosophy once they have engraved the ultimate knowledge into their minds.

'Upanishad' means 'vicinity of knowledge'. It relates to a student sitting near their teacher and to the Upanishad's knowledge closer to the Vedas. *'Adhyatma'* means the 'internal soul' or 'spiritual'. This Upanishad combines teachings from Shukla-Yajurveda and explores the inner divine presence. The prime soul is universal and omnipresent, but the beings bound by senses and ignorance are not aware of it. The material universe is an illusion which exists because of ego. Until ego is present in the body, one cannot realize this ultimate truth. The ignorant beings, trapped in material actions, remain in a loop of actions and consequences.

The Upanishad shows how losing desire for the material leads to liberation in life called 'living freedom'. How dedication to the singular and the universal destroys all past accumulated actions. It also mentions that one must face the past consequences at any cost but resolves the paradox by unveiling the soul's true form. The Upanishad asks the yogi to focus only on their soul and leave everything else. By realizing the soul within, one attains a *samadhi* 'balanced state' and becomes one with the ultimate soul.

Lord *Parashuram* is the teacher of this Upanishad, preaching about the eternal soul to his students. He had learned from his teacher *Raikva*, who learned from *Angiras*. *Angiras* learned from *Brahma* and *Brahma* learned it from *Apantaratam*. God, *Shiva*, taught this knowledge to *Apantaratam* first hand. Lord *Shiva* is the supreme God who creates, supports, and destroys the world. He has taught the art of yoga and other disciplines—which led to liberation— to several sages.

One needs self-study and speculation to realize the true meaning and implement it in life. It supplies invaluable help to students and individuals facing mid-life or late-life crisis. These old religious texts are appealing to those who are on a spiritual journey, seeking truth, or searching for purpose, including scientists.

J. Robert Oppenheimer, known for leading the Manhattan Project, learned Sanskrit to read the Bhagavad Gita. [Of Oppenheimer and the Bhagwat Gita (Lead, correcting intro) (April 22 is the 113th birth anniversary of Robert Oppenheimer). *The Economic Times. 22-April-2017*]

Erwin Schrödinger was the Nobel prize winner for physics in 1933. He wrote, "There is obviously only one alternative, namely the unification of minds or consciousnesses. Their multiplicity is only apparent. In truth, there is only one mind. This is the doctrine of the Upanishads." [Schrödinger, Erwin. What is life? Epilogue: On Determinism and Free Will]

Many others have found refuge in the scripture's wisdom. The Upanishads transcend common philosophy and impart eternal truth with scientific knowledge. All wise people must read it.

Contents

The Prayer for Peace

॥शांतिपाठः ॥

ॐ पूर्णमदः पूर्णमिदं पूर्णात्पूर्णमुदच्यते ।

पूर्णस्य पूर्णमादाय पूर्णमेवावशिष्यते ॥

ॐ शान्तिः शान्तिः शान्तिः ॥

Translation:

Om is whole in the beginning and is whole here. The wholesome of this universe takes birth from that singularity.

Remove the universe from singularity, and the remaining is still whole.

Om! Peace! Peace! Peace!

Comment:

Om is a universal entity—the consciousness of the universe. The Sanskrit word *'purna'* means 'complete', 'whole', or 'undivided singular'. It stays singular before the creation of the universe—like a black hole. Non-active, non-spatial, and timeless, it holds all elements— matter and energy, emotions, gods, and other beings. As an essence in the primitive state, upon creation, the universal soul weaves every quantum of the universe with itself. With the diversity of space and time, some of its factors become dominant and some suppressed on distinct occasions.

The *maya* 'world's apparent illusion' and ignorance (being's incapability) make the world seem diverse. However, the soul hides—as an abstract—in each particle, space, and time. Though diversified on the surface, the material universe is as complete and wholesome as the original soul is.

The verse further says that the ultimate soul is unexpendable. Even when the universe is born from a fragment of the universal consciousness, it remains undivided in its original abode. The soul does not diminish because everything comes from its spiritual essence. Such is the state of infinity. Infinity minus hundred or a googol is still infinity.

Adhyatma Upanishad

अन्तःशरिरे निहितो गुहायामज एको नित्यमस्य पृथिवी शरीरं यः पृथिवीमन्तरे संचरन्यं पृथिवी न वेद ।

यस्यापःशरीरं योऽपोऽन्तरे संचरन्यमापो न विदुः ।

यस्य तेजः शरीरं यस्तेजोऽन्तरे संचरन्यं तेजो न वेद ।

यस्य वायुः शरीरं यो वायुमन्तरे संचरन्यं वायुर्न वेद ।

यस्याकाशः शरीरं य आकाशमन्तरे संचरन्यमाकाशो न वेद ।

यस्य मनः शरीरं यो मनोऽन्तरे संचरन्यं मनो न वेद ।

यस्य बुद्धिः शरीरं यो बुद्धिमन्तरे संचरन्यं बुद्धिर्न वेद ।

यस्याहंकारः शरीरं योऽहंकारमन्तरे संचरन्यमहंकारो न वेद ।

यस्य चित्तं शरीरं यश्चित्तमन्तरे संचरन्यं चित्तं न वेद ।

यस्याव्यक्तं शरीरं योऽव्यक्तमन्तरे संचरन्यमव्यक्तं न वेद ।

यस्याक्षरं शरीरं योऽक्षरमन्तरे संचरन्यमक्षरं न वेद ।

यस्य मृत्युः शरीरं यो मृत्युमन्तरे संचरन्यं मृत्युर्न वेद ।
स एष सर्वभूतान्तरात्माऽपहतपाप्मा दिव्यो देव एको
नारायणः ।
अहं ममेति यो भावो देहाक्षादावनात्मनि ।
अध्यासोऽयं निरस्तव्यो विदुषा ब्रह्मनिष्ठया ॥ १ ॥

Translation:

Inside the body, the singular, continuous, and unborn exists in a cave.

Earth is its body. It roams inside the earth, but the earth does not know it.

Water is its body. It roams inside the water, but the water does not know it.

Fire is its body. It roams inside the fire, but the fire does not know it.

Air is its body. It roams inside the air, but the air does not know it.

Aether is its body. It roams inside the aether, but the aether does not know it.

Mind is its body. It roams inside the mind, but the mind does not know it.

Intelligence is its body. It roams inside the intelligence, but the intelligence does not know it.

Ego is its body. It roams inside the ego, but the ego does not know it.

Consciousness is its body. It roams inside the consciousness, but the consciousness does not know it.

Spiritual is its body. It roams inside the spiritual, but the spiritual does not know it.

Atom is its body. It roams inside the atom, but the atom does not know it.

Death is its body. It roams inside the death, but the death does not know it.

As the soul inside matter, it lies sin-free, and as the only god, *Narayana*.

'I' and 'mine' are the feelings of the body; and what the body can see is un-soulful.

The wise should obliterate this inferior, mythical knowledge with dedication towards the universal. — 1.

Comment:

The verse describes the soul's presence in the universe's elemental entities. It lives hidden, like in a cave.

Earth, water, fire, air, and aether are the universe's constituent elements. Nose, tongue, eyes, skin, and ears are the senses that perceive these elements. Reproductive, excretory, speech, locomotor (feet), and tactile (hands) organs are the senses that act on these elements. Smell, taste, light, touch, and sound are the objects of these senses. Apart from these, mind, intellect, ego, and consciousness are the internal senses. The ten senses, together with the four internal senses, operate, driven by the object's desire.

The soul uses these entities as faculties of operation, but they do not recognize their animator. *Narayana* is the true form of the universal soul—the soul of all matter, animate and inanimate. The ultimate deity rests in the infinite waters of oneness. The universe takes birth from it and returns to it in the end. Anything we can learn with our consciousness or perceive with our senses cannot tell the complete truth. Thus, the verse tells that the material universe is un-soulful. It recommends that we should strive towards the ultimate truth by discarding these material distractions.

Note: All physical entities like awareness, life, etc. which are unexpressed, are the spiritual entities.

The translation uses the word 'atom' as it better suits the undividable nature of akshar 'alphabet'.

***

ज्ञात्वा स्वं प्रत्यगात्मानं बुद्धितद्वृत्तिसाक्षिणम् ।

सोऽहमित्येव तद्वृत्त्या स्वान्यत्रात्ममतिं त्यजेत् ॥ २ ॥

Translation:

Know yourself as the image of the supreme, wilful soul. Think of yourself as the witness of intellect and its thoughts.

With the thought, "that is what I am", reject the idea of consciousness from all substances but you. — 2.

Comment:

This verse suggests thinking about oneself as the witness. The philosophy of "Who am I?" is old and famous, which the Upanishad answers with brilliance. A person is not their body or their emotions. They are not the summation of their experiences, too. Instead, they are the witness of these. The universal spirit in each being works with the five-perceptive, five-action, and the four internal senses. A person should regard only the soul as self. The rest are temporary tools to carry out actions in life.

The soul within a being lacks omnipotence and omniscience. However, by removing the impediments, one realizes that compartmentalization does not exist in a singular state. Thus, at the root level, the soul inside a being is the same as the universal soul.

Also, the knowledge of multiple souls is a fallacy. The true soul stays ever unfragmented. If nothing exists except one, how can there be a sense of mine, not mine, attraction, or repulsion? Thus, realizing the soul in oneself, a yogi rejects the idea of reality in anything else and quits engaging with the material.

***

लोकानुवर्तनं त्यक्त्वा त्यक्त्वा देहानुवर्तनम् ।
शास्त्रानुवर्तनं त्यक्त्वा स्वाध्यासापनयं कुरु ॥ ३ ॥

Translation:

Leave the maintenance of the world and leave the maintenance of the body.

Leave the maintenance of the scriptures and do not engage in the illusion of self. — 3.

Comment:

All material obligations are unnecessary, and one should discard anything that does not help the ultimate truth.

***

स्वात्मन्येव सदा स्थित्या मनो नश्यति योगिनः ।
युक्त्या श्रुत्या स्वानुभूत्या ज्ञात्वा सार्वात्म्यमात्मनः ॥ ४ ॥

Translation:

Establish yourself in your own resolute soul. Following the path of a yogi, your moodiness shall blemish.

Reason, listen, feel, and know your soul in every surrounding thing. — 4.

Comment:

Mind feeds on the objects of senses. It is a charioteer with five horses (five perceptive senses). Although the senses perceive the objects, the mind creates emotions. It causes the feelings of happiness, sadness, anger, and others. A yogi established in the soul stops listening to their mind. The associated feelings and emotions disappear, making them *sthita-pragya* 'firm-willed'. Insignificant disturbances in the surroundings do not affect them. Consequences do not matter. Prejudices and biases disappear, and the yogi sees the soul's truth in every surrounding thing. Thus, by dedicating thoughts and actions to the soul, the yogi overcomes their moodiness.

***

निद्राया लोकवार्तायाः शब्दादेरात्मविस्मृतेः ।
क्वचिन्नावसरं दत्त्वा चिन्तयात्मानमात्मनि ॥ ५ ॥

Translation:

Let not come the opportunity of sleep, worldly thoughts, objects of senses, and forgetfulness of the self.

Ruminate on the soul inside the soul. — 5.

Comment:

A minor mistake leads to a permanent veering off the path. A further explanation comes in the fifteenth verse. "Soul inside the soul" points to the universal soul inside the being's soul.

***

मातापित्रोर्मलोद्भूतं मलमांसमयं वपुः ।
त्यक्त्वा चण्डालवद्दूरं ब्रह्मभूय कृती भव ॥ ६ ॥

Translation:

Made from the dirt of parents, the body is full of flesh and excrement.

Distance it, like you distance a scavenger, and gratify yourself by being universal. — 6.

Comment:

The verse says that a being's body is the dirt of their parents. This is a popular philosophy about bodies in the Hindu religion. The soil becomes the food we eat, which then becomes us. Thus, the body is also soil. The same soil gives birth to another body, which accumulates more soil to grow.

Nothing is pious about a living-body. In the beginning, God *Vishnu* had killed two demons—*Madhu* and *Kaitabh*. Upon their death, their remains created the soil on earth. Since then, we call the earth by her name *Medini* 'made of flesh', and eating soil became a sin. Soil makes the human body, and soil it eats. The remains of demons and dead animals have submerged it. No baths, holy water, or prayers can putrefy a body of excrement, saliva, and pus.

Thus, the verse's advice is to discard the body like the society discards a *chandal* 'scavenger'. One cannot sever their body, but the verse asks to discard the activities which only satisfy the bodily needs. Only by realizing the universal truth, one overcomes the material illusion and thus gratifies themselves.

Note: Scavengers ate already dead animals and even dead humans, so, in ancient times, the society did not allow them in the civilization.

***

घटाकाशं महाकाश इवात्मानं परात्मनि ।
विलाप्याखण्डभावेन तूष्णीं भव सदा मुने ॥ ७ ॥

Translation:

Like we see aether in the space of objects, see the supreme god in the soul.

Immerse the soul in the universal spirit, with an unstaggering thought and be ever peaceful. — 7.

Comment:

Aether, together with the other four primary elements, makes up the matter in the universe. However, individual elements show their dominance in various objects. For example, in empty spaces (like between particles and outer space), aether is dominant. Similarly, air is present in the wind, fire is present in heat, electricity, etc. Water is present in all fluids, and earth is present in all solid objects.

The verse says that like we assume the element, aether, in an empty pot, we should assume the supreme god in our soul. Aether, although present across the universe, is not visible anywhere. So is the universal spirit hidden in all beings. Thus, meditating on the self, we immerse our soul in the ultimate being.

***

स्वप्रकाशमधिष्ठानं स्वयंभूय सदात्मना ।
ब्रह्माण्डमपि पिण्डाण्डं त्यज्यतां मलभाण्डवत् ॥ ८ ॥

Translation:

Be self-lit, resolute, self-existent, and ever soulful.

Discard the body and the universe like a pot of excrement. — 8.

Comment:

The verse asks to dedicate the mind and consciousness to the soul. One should not seek external objects for truth. With the belief that apart from the internal soul, the world is an illusion, one becomes self-existent and soulful. Only the soul is pious, the rest is an impure malice, a byproduct of our consciousness.

Thus, a yogi discards the universe along with their own body like an impure pot of excrement and accepts only the matters of soul.

***

चिदात्मनि सदानन्दे देहरूढामहंधियम् ।
निवेश्य लिङ्गमुत्सृज्य केवलो भव सर्वदा ॥ ९ ॥

Translation:

Direct the energy of material-inclined ego to the conscious and blissful soul.

Do not partake in the many that sprout from the material self and be the only ever. — 9.

Comment:

The mind and the ego cause an illusion of self. This illusion blankets the knowledge. One forgets that soul alone is the true being. The body and senses illude them into the material trap. This leads to a being investing in many activities sprouting from the illusionary self. A being takes countless forms to satisfy their self. They take many births, and in one birth they assume many positions. A son or a daughter, a spouse, a parent, a friend, or a foe are some of them. These relations sprout from the material bonds—temporary in the grandiose of time—but we engage in them with the utmost priority of our lives. In fact, these activities are artificial. Some help our livelihood, and some result from absolute vanity.

A yogi avoids worldly activities by logic. They sustain life, but do not take a dip in its muddy emotions and desires. Believing in oneself as the soul, one removes all masks of life. They become singular and take the path that takes them to the eternal destination. Hence, the verse suggests leaving the infinite illusions of self and being the one soul that unites the universe and beyond.

***

यत्रैष जगदाभासो दर्पणान्तःपुरं यथा ।
तद्ब्रह्माहमिति ज्ञात्वा कृतकृत्यो भवानघ ॥ १० ॥

Translation:

Like one knows the world by looking at a city in a mirror.

Gratify yourself by knowing the universe in the soul. — 10.

Comment:

A mirror is tiny compared to a city, just as a soul is insignificant compared to the universal soul. However, one sees the entire city's reflection in a small mirror. Similarly, a being's soul is apt for realizing the universal soul.

Once a yogi realizes they are a part of the supreme God, none of the worldly actions stay a priority. They believe in the thought, "I have seen what I had to see and done what I had to do". Their actions stem from the universal will, not nature's forces. This state of acting, free from anticipating the consequences, is gratification.

Note: God Brahma took birth from the lotus like navel of Vishnu. He created the nature and its forces, sat, raj, and tam. Curiosity, truth, and empathy are the deeds of sat. Venture, ambition, and anger are the deeds of raj, and laziness, falsehood, and addiction are the deeds of tam. The trio influence all beings in some combination, and no one can escape any of them. A yogi learns to balance them with equality, which leads to a stabilized mind. With a dedicated mind, desires suppress, and one gains control of their senses. Without the haphazard senses' disturbance, the yogi realizes the soul.

***

अहंकारग्रहान्मुक्तः स्वरूपमुपपद्यते ।
चन्द्रवद्विमलः पूर्णः सदानन्दः स्वयंप्रभः ॥ ११ ॥

Translation:

Free from ego, one realizes the true form of self.

Like the moon, they become complete, ever blissful, and self-lit. — 11.

Comment:

When a being suffers from illusionary ego, their position in the world becomes the same as an inanimate object. Instead of showing intelligence, they become dull as a dodo. Their actions do not take them anywhere. Their thoughts are a waste. However, once a yogi overcomes their ego, they realize, and so assume, the same position as the supreme soul.

The verse compares the state with the moon. The moon's light is bright enough to scare the dark away, but cool enough to give the vegetation the best growth. Similarly, the enlightened person acts in the world but becomes free of emotional impurities like anger, hatred, etc. They become complete and ever blissful.

Note: The Hindu scriptures say that although the sun is vital for life, the moon also plays a significant role. Without the moon's light, none of the vegetation would survive. They say the moon rains a special ambrosia that nurtures the aushadhi 'vegetation' on earth. Science reaffirms this point as the recent discoveries point to several botanical activities taking place only in the night.

The verse mentions the moon to be self-lit, which contradicts the modern science. Remember that the Upanishads take a spiritual perspective of explaining the physical events. Philosophically speaking, even the sun includes borrowed material. Hence, nothing in the universe is self-sustaining. Also, moon's light and sun's light have tremendous differences. While the sun is hot, the moon is cold—a full moon night is colder than a no moon night on earth. Hence, we can assume the Upanishads have considered the moon's light more than just a reflection.

***

क्रियानाशाद्भवेच्चिन्तानाशोऽस्माद्वासनाक्षयः ।
वासनाप्रक्षयो मोक्षः सा जीवन्मुक्तिरिष्यते ॥ १२ ॥

Translation:

Abstinence from worldly activities eliminates worries. Without worries, desires decimate.

The end of desires is salvation, also called "living freedom". — 12.

Comment:

This verse shows the activities leading to salvation. Salvation comes in many forms, some after the universe's end, some after death, and some in life. 'Living freedom' is a salvation which a yogi can achieve in life. In this salvation, the yogi continues their livelihood, but the consequences (sins and virtues) do not attach to them. Their actions become free of desires and emotions, and their will becomes one with the will of God.

***

सर्वत्र सर्वतः सर्वब्रह्ममात्रावलोकनम् ।
सद्भावभावनादाढर्याद्धासनालयमश्नुते ॥ १३ ॥

Translation:

One who always sees only the soul in everything.

One whose emotions and will have become resolute; their desires diminish; such is the saying in the Vedas. — 13.

***

प्रमादो ब्रह्मनिष्ठायां न कर्तव्यः कदाचन ।
प्रमादो मृत्युरित्याहुर्विद्यायां ब्रह्मवादिनः ॥ १४ ॥

Translation:

Never be careless in dedication to the soul.

The wise who speak of the universe have said that carelessness is the same as death. — 14.

***

यथाऽपकृष्टं शैवालं क्षणमात्रं न तिष्ठति ।
आवृणोति तथा माया प्राज्ञं वापि पराङ्मुखम् ॥ १५ ॥

Translation:

When you rake away the algae in a pond, it does not stay back afterwards, even for a moment.

Likewise, *maya* blankets the will the moment one looks away from the soul. — 15.

Comment:

The verses 14 and 15 show why dedication and resolution are important for salvation. Although the soul is pure and supreme, it lives in a body made of senses. Our ignorance and the world's *maya* 'illusion' create falsehoods which make a being act only to enjoy the pleasures and avoid the material pain. A being is bound by their senses, emotions, and impulses. Hence, one moment's carelessness leads to an entire rupture of the realization, and the person falls from grace.

We saw in the twelfth verse how avoiding worldly desires escalates a being towards salvation. Similarly, one carefree mistake torpedoes a person back into the spirals of ignorance. Again, the yogi must go through the penances and austerities to re-attain their former state. In fact, they might not get a second chance. Thus, a yogi should avoid carelessness at all costs.

***

जीवतो यस्य कैवल्यं विदेहोऽपि स केवलः ।
समाधिनिष्ठतामेत्य निर्विकल्पो भवानघ ॥ १६ ॥

Translation:

One who has attained *kaivalya* in life will leave the body and remain only as the soul.

Hence, o sin-less, be immutable in the dedication towards *samadhi*. — 16.

Comment:

Kaivalya 'living freedom' is the salvation discussed earlier. *Samadhi* is the last stage of a yogi's journey. In this stage, they become one with the soul. Salvation's attainment happens through yoga's eight organs:

Yama **'control'**: Restricting oneself only to the righteous actions like non-violence, truth, etc.

Niyama **'discipline'**: Following the disciplines of hygiene, contentment, austerities, etc.

Asana **'seat'**: Sitting for a long time with calmness and without disturbances—physical and mental.

Pranayama **'breath-control'**: Controlling the breath by inhaling, holding, and exhaling in calculated times.

Pratyahara **'alternate feeding'**: Leaving the desires created by the senses. Abstaining from the objects like smell, taste, etc. Instead, satisfying the senses by yields of the soul.

Dharana **'grasp'**: Imagining God in oneself and seeing the universal reflection in one's body.

Dhyana **'meditation'**: Meditating on the supreme soul.

Samadhi **'self's balance'**: Realizing the supreme soul, knowing the universe's truth, and becoming one with it.

***

अज्ञानहृदयग्रन्थेर्निःशेषविलयस्तदा ।
समाधिनाऽविकल्पेन यदाऽद्वैतात्मदर्शनम् ॥ १७ ॥

Translation:

Ignorance in the arteries of the heart disappears.

As soon as one realizes the non-dual soul in an immutable *samadhi*. — 17.

Comment:

The verse uses the word *advaita* 'non-dual' for the soul. The universal soul appears dual in the material world as God and the being. However, a yogi knows that at the root level, they are the same. The being's soul exists only until maya has blanketed the ultimate knowledge. After enlightenment, soul dilutes in soul and the duality disappears. Everything becomes one and complete.

अत्रात्मत्वं दृढीकुर्वन्नहमादिषु संत्यजन् ।
उदासीनतया तेषु तिष्ठेद्घटपटादिवत् ॥ १८ ॥

Translation:

With resolution in the internal soul, discard everything, including ego, etc.

Be neutral as one does, towards discarding clothes and utensils, etc. — 18.

Comment:

The verse suggests discarding all emotions and desires. While doing so, one should not feel loss or guilt. A person who takes the life of asceticism by force, but craves worldly luxuries, is worse than one who does not walk this path. Hence, first, one must affirm their will and dedication towards God. With practice, they build a nature that finds bliss in the soul alone. The material luxuries seem mundane, emotions seldom have high amplitudes, and the mind becomes a windless flame. When this happens, a yogi leaves the dependence on the sense's objects, like one discards old clothes and utensils.

***

ब्रह्मादिस्तम्बपर्यन्तं मृषामात्रा उपाधयः ।
ततः पूर्णं स्वमात्मानं पश्येदेकात्मना स्थितम् ॥ १९ ॥

Translation:

From *Brahma* to a blade of grass, all positions are illusion.

Hence, visualize only the internal soul, which is singular in all states. — 19.

Comment:

The verse states that Brahma's position is as illusory as a blade of grass. A yogi should discard not only the earthly desires but ambitions of even heavens. All worldly positions result from byproducts of creation. Better offers cannot cheat a person who understands that the soul is indivisible.

Thus, a yogi should only aim for the supreme soul, which is the ultimate state of all beings.

***

स्वयं ब्रह्मा स्वयं विष्णुः स्वयमिन्द्रः स्वयं शिवः ।
स्वयं विश्वमिदं सर्वं स्वस्मादन्यन्न किंचन ॥ २० ॥

Translation:

Self is *Brahma*, self is *Vishnu*, self is *Indra*, self is *Shiva*.

Self is the world, and self is everything. Except for self, nothing exists. — 20.

Comment:

In this verse, 'self' is not the illusion of self, but the pure universal soul present in all beings.

Brahma is the creator of the universe, who exists as the literal universe in the present day.

Vishnu supports the world and keeps it in its propriety. He is present in every bit of space. He is the reason the space expands as the word '*Vishnu*' means "which fills (spreads in all directions)".

Indra is the king of the gods, who is also a form of *Vishnu*. He dominates the natural phenomena. He brings rains and thunder. Other gods, by his permission, rule the winds, sun, moon, and others. Also, he is the ruler of the senses in living beings.

Shiva is the supreme god who is eternal. The universe collapses on his command to be one with him again. The supreme soul is beyond imagination and beyond explanation.

However, the scriptures interpret it in five forms. They are the five chief gods in Hinduism. These gods also exist as demigods, but because of their prime presence in the universe, the sages believe them to be self-born and self-derived. They are *Surya-Narayan (Brahma)*, *Maha-Vishnu*, *Maha-Rudra (Shiva)*, *Maha-Devi (Adya-Shakti)*, and *Maha-Ganesh*.

Thus, the supreme soul is present as all gods. Since the same soul is present in human beings, self too, is the same as the gods. *Jabal-Darshan-Upanishad* says, "Looking for gods in idols and objects is like picking up dirt and leaving the gold".

Apart from this, the Upanishads have also described the symbolic places of all gods, sacred physical events, and pilgrimages in our body. If we can worship their symbols in temples, rituals, and books, we can worship them in the body, too. Hence, we should only look for the soul within ourselves.

***

स्वात्मन्यारोपिता शेषाभासवस्तुनिरासतः ।
स्वयमेव परंब्रह्म पूर्णमद्वयमक्रियम् ॥ २१ ॥

Translation:

Like the illusion of a snake in a rope, perceiving objects in one's consciousness is imaginary.

Self is the prime soul, complete, non-dual, and inactive. — 21.

Comment:

In low light, our subconscious fear of snakes makes us see one in a rope. Similarly, with less knowledge, our consciousness makes us see a variety of objects in the universe.

According to Upanishads' philosophy, objects in the universe only exist with consciousness. Rigidity, density, colors, gravity, etc. exist only as relative entities. Without a conscious being that compares them in various locations and times, they do not exist. Thus, half the physics we study is only real if conscious beings study it. The other half, which talks about the objective truths, are also an illusion.

~ 26 ~

Matter has quantum sized constituents (theorized as strings) which exist in a high energy state. They come together to create atoms, molecules, and visible objects. A little thinking reveals that this classification is a comparative scale. If one composition is the truth, the other is a myth.

Atoms make up all objects. Hence, we can describe the universe only as atoms. This makes the existence of objects an illusion of consciousness. Same is true for the atoms if the universe's truth is subatomic particles, and so on. In fact, the entire universe is just one big energy field—the singular, complete apocalyptic water.

Consciousness is the root of the illusion we see in the universe. It creates fake classification and diversity. We cannot formulate the infinite universe. However, we can always find the complete, non-dual, and inactive soul within ourselves.

***

असत्कल्पो विकल्पोऽयं विश्वमित्येकवस्तुनि ।
निर्विकारे निराकारे निर्विशेषे भिदा कुतः ॥ २२ ॥

Translation:

'One' and 'many' are false and illusionary is the world.

How can there be fragments in the pure, formless, and propertyless? — 22.

***

द्रष्टृदर्शनदृश्यादिभावशून्ये निरामये ।
कल्पार्णव इवात्यन्तं परिपूर्णे चिदात्मनि ॥ २३ ॥

Translation:

It is free from seer, seeing, and sight and is impurity free.

It is complete, conscious, and soulful, like the apocalyptic water. — 23.

Comment:

Seer, seeing, and sight are the variations that create diversity. If soul alone exits, none of these are true.

The apocalyptic water absorbs everything at the end of time. All beings together with their life-forces, senses, and elements exist as an essence in that water. Unlike the water you see on earth, the eternal water is conscious, soulful, and complete. Such is the soul's true form.

***

तेजसीव तमो यत्र विलीनं भ्रान्तिकारणम् ।
अद्वितीये परे तत्त्वे निर्विशेषे भिदा कुतः ॥ २४ ॥

Translation:

Like darkness disappears into light, the reason
for illusion disappears into the non-dual soul.

That prime, para-universal element is inactive,
so how can it have any variations? — 24.

***

एकात्मके परे तत्त्वे भेदकर्ता कथं वसेत् ।
सुषुप्तौ सुखमात्रायां भेदः केनावलोकितः ॥ २५ ॥

Translation:

How can segmentation happen in the singular
element?

Deep sleep is blissful. Who has seen activity in it?
— 25.

***

चित्तमूलो विकल्पोऽयं चित्ताभावे न कश्चन ।
अतश्चित्तं समाधेहि प्रत्यग्रूपे परात्मनि ॥ २६ ॥

Translation:

Consciousness is the root cause of diversity. Without consciousness, variety does not exist.

Hence, fix your consciousness in *samadhi* to the image of the resolute soul. — 26.

Comment:

Verse 21's comment covers the descriptions for the verses 24, 25, and 26. The rest is for self-study and inspection.

***

अखण्डानन्दमात्मानं विज्ञाय स्वस्वरूपतः ।
बहिरन्तः सदानन्दरसास्वादनमात्मनि ॥ २७ ॥

Translation:

Know the undivided, blissful soul in your own self.

From outside and inside, drink the eternal bliss from your soul. — 27.

Comment:

This verse reiterates to find the supreme soul within oneself. It further suggests drinking its bliss from outside and inside. An unenlightened person depends on the external objects for satisfying their five perceptive senses. They depend on internal emotions to satisfy their internal senses of mind, intellect, consciousness, and ego. However, once a yogi finds the soul within themselves, both the external and internal satisfactions come only from it.

***

वैराग्यस्य फलं बोधो बोधस्योपरतिः फलम् ।
स्वानन्दानुभवाच्छान्तिरेषैवोपरतेः फलम् ॥ २८ ॥

Translation:

Reclusion leads to knowledge, knowledge leads to substinence.

Substinence leads to peace by reaching a bliss of the soul. — 28.

Comment:

When a yogi dedicates their consciousness to the soul, they turn reclusive towards the material luxuries. Instead of wandering in search of temporary wealth, reclusion leads to a better use of the mind and intellect. It reveals knowledge about the universe and the soul. The knowledge causes the desires of the yogi to subside, causing substinence from the objects of senses. A substinent person becomes resolute in an unhindered dedication to the soul. The soul's dedication brings eternal bliss and peace to the yogi.

Note: These are the added benefits that result from actions while realizing the truth. However, they are not the ultimate motive for a yogi. They walk the path only for salvation.

***

यद्युत्तरोत्तराभावे पूर्वपूर्वं तु निष्फलम् ।
निवृत्तिः परमा तृप्तिरानन्दोऽनुपमः स्वतः ॥ २९ ॥

Translation:

If the latter in these are not there, the former are useless.

Substinence is the ultimate satisfaction, and the bliss of the soul is incomparable. — 29.

Comment:

This verse clarifies that reclusion is not effective without knowledge. A rock without self-knowledge is not enlightened, just reclusive. Hence, a yogi must try that reclusion leads to knowledge. Similarly, a knowledgeable person who still indulges in the desires is hypocritical and wastes away their life. Finally, a reclusive person who has knowledge and lives by substinence must find peace and bliss in the soul. Melancholy is not sustainable for a yogi's life. If a person is not blissful with their own soul, they are neither knowledgeable nor have reached a state of neutrality.

Thus, substinence should be satisfying for a yogi, and the bliss of the soul should be incomparable to any other pleasures in the world.

***

मायोपाधिर्जगद्योनिः सर्वज्ञत्वादिलक्षणः ।
पारोक्ष्यशबलः सत्याद्यात्मकस्तत्पदाभिधः ॥ ३० ॥

Translation:

Known by the name *'maya'*, the universe's seed has properties of omniscience, etc.

Mysteriously powerful, and the truth in the world, it secures the position of *'tat'*. — 30.

Comment:

The universal spirit creates the world, and hence, is the birthplace of the universe. It creates a world of mystery by trapping the beings in a material body. We only understand the illusion the soul creates while its true form always stays hidden. Thus, the soul assumes the position of *maya* in this world. Although omnipotent, its power is not apparent (because of its hidden nature) and is a mystery for the living. The hidden soul is true at all places and times. Thus, the universe becomes God's manifestation, which the verse calls *tat* 'that'.

***

आलम्बनतया भाति योऽस्मत्प्रत्ययशब्दयोः ।
अन्तःकरणसंभिन्नबोधः स त्वंपदाभिधः ॥ ३१ ॥

Translation:

Which depends on the affixes of 'me'.

Which seems diverse to the internal senses; that being is called '*tvam*'. — 31.

Comment:

The ego, consciousness, and mind make a being believe in a diversity of things. Some things, the being calls 'I'. The body, along with its thoughts and emotions, is what the being thinks of themselves. Other things it calls 'mine'. Death of a spouse or a child becomes the being's death. Similarly, wealth becomes as lovely as an organ to some people. A person is their body, their family, and their wealth. Hence, all the identities that the being denotes as 'I' is what the verse calls '*tvam*' 'you'.

***

मायाविद्ये विहायैव उपाधी परजीवयोः ।
अखण्डं सच्चिदानन्दं परं ब्रह्म विलक्ष्यते ॥ ३२ ॥

Translation:

Remove maya and ignorance from the world and the being.

Only the undivided, true, wilful, blissful, metaphysical, and universal soul remains. — 32.

***

इत्थं वाक्यैस्तदर्थानुसन्धानं श्रवणं भवेत् ।
युक्त्या संभावितत्वानुसन्धानं मननं तु तत् ॥ ३३ ॥

Translation:

To reason and understand the meaning of the sentence *"tat-tvam-asi"* is the only communion.

To implement the words with reason is the only contemplation. — 33.

Comment:

Here, the verse emphasizes on the rituals of religion. All rituals that end up in material benefits are shun-worthy. *Tat-tvam-asi* 'that is what you are' is the resolving sentence of the Vedas. We have seen that 'that' means the universe, and 'you' means what we call as 'I' and 'mine'. Thus, this significant Vedic sentence says that the being is the universe.

This verse suggests that nothing, but this principle is worthy of listening. Other principles that talk about the temporary, material theories are vain and useless. Thinking about the meaning of *'tat-tvam-asi'* and how to implement it into action is the only contemplation. All other worries, plans, and ruminations are a waste of time.

***

ताभ्यां निर्विचिकित्सेऽर्थे चेतसः स्थापितस्य यत् ।
एकतानत्वमेतद्धि निदिध्यासनमुच्यते ॥ ३४ ॥

Translation:

Free your consciousness from doubts and fix it on the substance.

Thus, attain a resonance between communion and contemplation. This is called the 'continuous meditative state'. — 34.

Comment:

This verse describes the steps of *samadhi*. When thoughts and actions come on the same plane, a continuous meditative state emerges. In normal conditions, a yogi attains *samadhi* in a seated position. They leave actions to practice *parent* 'breath-control', *dharana* 'imagination', and *dhyana* 'meditation'. However, when the yogi learns the art of control in actions, they are in a *samadhi* while performing worldly actions as well.

***

ध्यातृध्याने परित्यज्य क्रमाद्ध्येयैकगोचरम् ।
निवातदीपवच्चित्तं समाधिरभिधीयते ॥ ३५ ॥

Translation:

Afterwards, leaving the thought of the contemplator and the contemplation, fix your mind on the contemplative.

Samadhi is when consciousness becomes tranquil, like a windless flame. — 35.

Comment:

After one finds a resonance between thoughts and actions, they overcome *maya*. The feeling of 'I' disappears, and the contemplator ceases to exist. The being's soul dissolves into God. Thoughts disappear, as thoughts are a product of mind. With the being's mind, ego, and consciousness dissolving into the universal unity, where is the question of contemplation? Only the contemplative or the supreme spirit exists, and with it, the yogi reaches the eternal, blissful state. This is *samadhi*.

***

वृत्तयस्तु तदानीमप्यज्ञाता आत्मगोचराः ।
स्मरणादनुमीयन्ते व्युत्थितस्य समुत्थिताः ॥ ३६ ॥

Translation:

In the state of samadhi, the soul only acknowledges the objects of senses, but they do not materialize.

When a yogi wakes up from samadhi, they can recall those experiences and feelings from memory. — 36.

Comment:

This verse explains the state of *samadhi*. A yogi encounters the objects of senses, like one knows their dreams. They hear the sounds and see the world, but the emotions associated with these feelings do not arise. The yogi is not afraid of risks in an action. They are not happy with success or exasperated after failure. They can tell sweet from bitter, but their ascension pulls them away from liking or disliking the taste. A yogi carries out the body's duties to sustain life, because their presence in the world is a reality. However, they do not desire to extend or end it in want of another destination.

The material interactions are the deeds of *maya*. Hence, waking up from *samadhi*, those events seem like illusionary dreams. A yogi remembers them but knows they were fake. Such is the state of supreme knowledge.

***

अनादाविह संसारे संचिताः कर्मकोटयः ।
अनेन विलयं यान्ति शुद्धो धर्मो विवर्धते ॥ ३७ ॥

Translation:

In the unending universe, millions of actions assemble.

However, with *samadhi*, those actions vanish, and *dharma* multiplies. — 37

Comment:

When we live, we perform actions. All actions lead to consequences. Our actions affect others and other actions affect us. In an infinite amount of time, consequences travel an extensive network to return to its origin. The law of actions and their consequences is *'dharma'* in Sanskrit.

In a stint of time, we see randomness in cause and effect—our virtuous deeds yield painful experiences and vice versa. However, the mysterious truth is far from what we can fathom. The universe keeps a track of all interactions. At some place, a rock strikes another rock. After many rebirths, the second rock becomes the sword that strikes the first rock, now a piece of wood. The scriptures state that the law is too complex for anyone—even the wisest of sages—to comprehend.

When *Brahma* was born from the lotus like navel of *Vishnu*, he landed in an infinity of nothing. Baffled and confused, in an instant, he had realized the illusion of the world and the absence of bliss in it. He wanted to return to be one with the soul. He prayed to *Vishnu* and *Vishnu* told him that the only way back was through. So *Brahma* created the universe and filled it with divine and mortal beings. The conscious beings' illusion led to the creation of new actions. Their moodiness made their actions haphazard, creating even more actions and attracting more consequences.

This is how the actions expand the universe. This is the reason *Brahma* creates beings to return to his abode. All beings become only the tool in the hands of a much larger *dharma* to continue the universe's fixed path.

The scriptures suggest a selfish approach while dealing with this problem. All events are the deeds of nature. Our ignorance and the absence of knowledge makes us believe we are the free willed actors. A yogi who knows this does not interfere in the grand plan or tries to change its course—because it is impossible. They adapt and accept their nature and act with the will of the supreme soul. They worry only about themselves and leave the world to its own fate. Once a yogi attains samadhi, they dissolve in the supreme will, and hence the ego of being an actor disappears. Without action, how can there be consequences? Hence, the enlightened yogi becomes a non-actor while carrying out their duties in life. He lets others be as they are, sees their vicious cycles of actions and consequences, but does nothing to correct it. Because corrections arise from the ego of duality.

Also, any new actions of the yogi vanish. They live in a balanced state, hence do not make foolish mistakes. They keep in mind the laws of the nature and act only for sustenance. Thus, their *dharma* multiplies. They get austere powers, but without using them for material benefits, they continue the path of non-action. In the end, when they leave the world, they do not return. Their consciousness doesn't transfer to another body. Dissolving in the supreme spirit, they themselves become the supreme god.

***

धर्ममेघमिमं प्राहुः समाधिं योगवित्तमाः ।
वर्षत्येष यथा धर्मामृतधाराः सहस्रशः ॥ ३८ ॥

Translation:

Superior people call this *samadhi 'dharma megha'*.

Because thousands of streams of *dharma* rains on the yogi. — 38.

Comment:

The stage right before *samadhi* is of *dharma megha* 'cloud of righteousness'. In this state, the magnitude of the revealed knowledge compares to that of a heavy precipitation.

When the yogi becomes one with the supreme spirit, the superior knowledge reveals itself unto them. They discover the secrets of the universe, as they build new neural connections which are impossible for a person engaged in the deeds of the material. This knowledge is not a hunch or a spiritual revelation. It comes to them like one knows language.

This strength makes the yogi see the laws and theories like one sees colors. Even without reading or knowing the scriptures, they take the right path. Their intuitive decisions become more precise than other's calculated and meditated plans. They choose right from wrong in their heart and never stagger on their path.

Without this stage of knowledge, one cannot achieve *kaivalya* 'living freedom'.

***

अमुना वासनाजाले निःशेषं प्रविलापिते ।
समूलोन्मूलिते पुण्यपापाख्ये कर्मसंचये ॥ ३९ ॥

Translation:

Through this *samadhi*, the desires absolve in entirety.

The actions with properties of virtues and sins vanish with their roots. — 39.

***

वाक्यमप्रतिबद्धं सत्प्राक्परोक्षावभासिते ।
करामलकवद्बोधपरोक्षं प्रसूयते ॥ ४० ॥

Translation:

Bound by the words, first the hidden knowledge reveals.

Then, the universe's knowledge comes like the exfoliation of hands. — 40.

Comment:

A clarification of the verses 39 and 40 has come earlier. "The exfoliation of hand" implies that samadhi's knowledge is not just theoretical, but tangible and genuine. It also signifies that the knowledge comes from within, and one does not have to go places or work on other objects.

***

वासनानुदयो भोग्ये वैराग्यस्य तदावधिः ।
अहंभावोदयाभावो बोधस्य परमावधिः ॥ ४१ ॥

Translation:

When the emotion of the desire does not erupt, even in the presence of desirable objects, then know it as the ultimate state of detachment.

When the emotion of pride does not come, even in a situation of pride, then know it as the ultimate state of knowledge. — 41.

Comment:

Detachment and a loss of ego are easy if no circumstances arise for their show. Until death, a person may never encounter their ego. A person who has no wealth would seem like a detached person. However, one should test their cognizance only when tempting situations arise. Test yourself and find out if you are ready for the ultimate knowledge.

***

लीनवृत्तेरनुत्पत्तिर्मर्यादोपरतेस्तु सा ।
स्थितप्रज्ञो यतिरयं यः सदानन्दमश्नुते ॥ ४२ ॥

Translation:

When the maleficent feelings do not arise, know it as the state of substinence.

A person in this state is called *sthita-pragya*, who is ever blissful. — 42.

Comment:

Sthita-pragya 'firm-willed', as discussed earlier, is the state where the yogi has found a balance between actions and thoughts. No amount of temptation hinders their beliefs. They have left all desires and emotions behind. They have lost their individual ego and identify only as the supreme soul.

***

ब्रह्मण्येव विलीनात्मा निर्विकारो विनिष्क्रियः ।
ब्रह्मात्मनोः शोधितयोरेकभावावगाहिनि ॥ ४३ ॥

Translation:

The malice-free diffusion into the soul vanquishes all actions.

Realization of the soul makes the feelings and speech singular. — 43.

निर्विकल्पा च चिन्मात्रा वृत्तिः प्रज्ञेति कथ्यते ।
सा सर्वदा भवेद्यस्य स जीवन्मुक्त इष्यते ॥ ४४ ॥

Translation:

Such a pure consciousness is called a wilful conscience.

When a wilful conscience is always present in a person, that state is called 'living freedom'. — 44.

Comment:

The verses 43 and 44 emphasize on the importance of resonance between the thoughts and the actions. Only when the feelings (thoughts) and the speech (action) become singular should one say they have attained *samadhi*.

After reading a few books, the mind may create illusionary knowledge. For such people, thoughts, speech, and actions are incongruent. They are confused. On the surface, they use reason and logic to understand the scripture's principles, but their actions show otherwise. The fact is, one cannot understand these principles with intellect because the soul's knowledge is beyond the senses. In the first verse, we have seen examples like, "Intellect is its body. It roams in the intellect, but the intellect does not know it", etc.

For example, a fat person may want to eat a cake, but reasons and denies the offer. On a second thought, they may taste it with a small bite. In this example, the person's will originated from desire, their speech was ideal, and action balanced. The disturbances in emotions corrupt such will.

One may say that they have reached the zenith of knowledge only if their actions and thoughts become resonant. The mind becomes free of secret desires. Hypocrisy disappears, and thoughts convert to speech and actions. This is the true will of a person. When such a will becomes firm and never goes away, the person attains living freedom (salvation).

In the next verses, we will see more definitions of the salvation, called 'living freedom'.

***

देहेन्द्रियेष्वहंभाव इदंभावस्तदन्यके ।
यस्य नो भवतः क्वापि स जीवन्मुक्त इष्यते ॥ ४५ ॥

Translation:

One feels pride (the knowledge of self) in their body and senses, and pride (possessiveness) in other things.

When this feeling never comes, that state is called 'living freedom'. — 45.

***

न प्रत्यग्ब्रह्मणोर्भेदं कदापि ब्रह्मसर्गयोः ।
प्रज्ञया यो विजानाति स जीवन्मुक्त इष्यते ॥ ४६ ॥

Translation:

No difference exists between people and God, and God and the universe.

Who is conscientious about this attains the state called 'living freedom'. — 46.

***

साधुभिः पूज्यमानेऽस्मिन्पीडचमानेऽपि दुर्जनैः ।
समभावो भवेद्यस्य स जीवन्मुक्त इष्यते ॥ ४७ ॥

Translation:

Even when worshiped by saints, and even when abused by hoodlums.

When a person is unhindered by their emotions, that state is called 'living freedom'. — 47.

***

विज्ञातब्रह्मतत्त्वस्य यथापूर्वं न संसृतिः ।
अस्ति चेन्न स विज्ञातब्रह्मभावो बहिर्मुखः ॥ ४८ ॥

Translation:

One who gains the universal knowledge does not look at the world in the same way as before.

So, if a person sees the world as before, understand they do not have the universal knowledge, and they look outward for their beliefs. — 48.

Comment:

The soul's knowledge changes our outlook. Things that attracted us before become irrational. The undercooked myth becomes the harsh reality. If a person processes thoughts the same way, even after enlightenment, their knowledge is an illusion. A trick of the mind, such knowledge is *maya*.

The verse uses the word *bahirmukh* 'outward facing', which is one of the two methods of inspection. When a person looks at the physical events to understand the secrets of the universe, they are outward facing for answers. All modern scientists are the examples. With this method, we develop useful resources, invent technology, and make our lives easier.

Outward facing knowledge helps survival, but is meaningless in a repetitive world. The scriptures have said that superior knowledge comes when the person is inward facing. Inward facing knowledge teaches about the spiritual, universal truths, and righteousness in actions. With this knowledge, life may be short or long, secure, or risky, but is peaceful and satisfactory. Also, it helps in breaking the cycles of rebirths through salvation.

Hence, the verse says that knowledge that focuses on the material aspects of the world does not lead to salvation. The supreme knowledge will uproot the standing priorities and change the person from within.

***

सुखाद्यनुभवो यावत्तावत्प्रारब्धमिष्यते ।
फलोदयः क्रियापूर्वो निष्क्रियो नहि कुत्रचित् ॥ ४९ ॥

Translation:

Until feelings like happiness exist, think of them as consequences of the past.

All fruits result from previous actions. Without actions, consequences do not exist. — 49.

***

अहं ब्रह्मेति विज्ञानात्कल्पकोटिशतार्जितम् ।
संचितं विलयं याति प्रबोधात्स्वप्नकर्मवत् ॥ ५० ॥

Translation:

The knowledge of 'I am the universal soul' ends the consequential actions of all past lives.

Same as actions of a dream disappear after waking up. — 50.

Comment:

The verses 49 and 50 say that all feelings arise as the consequences of actions (from the illusion of being an actor). Hence, until emotions exist, one has not attained liberation. However, later verses reveal that a liberated person is not exempt from consequences. Liberation does not isolate the body from the universe, only the soul. Hence, *samadhi* ends all actions to diminish emotions and desires, but not pain and pleasure.

The fiftieth verse compares the actions with events of a dream. Like actions performed in dream are fake, actions in the material world are also fake. If one drinks water in a dream, it does not quench the thirst in the real world. The snake bite in the dream does not poison their organs. After waking up, the actions disappear, and so do they after liberation.

However, remnants of dream exist even after waking up. If one sees an attacking tiger in the dream, the fear stays after they wake up. Likewise, consequences of the past actions bear fruits even after liberation.

स्वमसङ्गमुदासीनं परिज्ञाय नभो यथा ।
न श्लिष्यते यतिः किंचित्कदाचिद्भाविकर्मभिः ॥ ५१ ॥

Translation:

Like the sky is self-indulgent and neutral with the activities on earth.

A yogi never engages in worldly actions. — 51.

Comment:

The sounds, winds, etc. stop at the boundary of atmosphere and do not affect the sky. The sky, too, although supports the celestial bodies, never engages in their activities. Similarly, a yogi witnesses everything but does not malign themselves with the actions of the material.

This verse conveys a different meaning with sky's meaning as 'aether'. Aether stays pure even after being inside all objects. The Hindu scriptures say that aether created air, air created fire, fire created water, and water created earth. Each former element is present in its creation. Thus, aether is present in all elements, but it also exists alone, unaffected by others. It exists within itself and does not need interactions to sustain its life.

Note: Two atoms can come close to a minimum of 10^{-8} meters. Beyond this, if they come closer, there would be a nuclear reaction. So far, whatever we have discovered (molecules, atoms, subatomic particles, etc.), *some inter particle space is always present. Hence, aether is not only present in the outer space but also in the inter-atomic spaces on earth. The atoms affect each other, but not the space in between.*

***

न नभो घटयोगेन सुरागन्धेन लिप्यते ।
तथाऽऽत्मोपाधियोगेन तद्धर्मेर्नैव लिप्यते ॥ ५२ ॥

Translation:

Alcohol's smell does not affect the sky in its pot.

Likewise, the soul, even after living in the body, does not gain its properties. — 52.

Comment:

Here again, the sky is not the space with air—the smell affects the air but not the inter-atomic space.

***

ज्ञानोदयात्पुराऽऽरब्धं कर्म ज्ञानान्न नश्यति ।
अदत्त्वा स्वफलं लक्ष्यमुद्दिश्योत्सृष्टबाणवत् ॥ ५३ ॥

Translation:

The knowledge and actions, limited to the body, disappear after enlightenment.

Like a released arrow is sure bound for the target, the deeds before enlightenment surely bear fruits. — 53.

**

व्याघ्रबुद्ध्या विनिर्मुक्तो बाणः पश्चात्तु गोमतौ ।
न तिष्ठति भिनत्त्येव लक्ष्यं वेगेन निर्भरम् ॥ ५४ ॥

Translation:

An arrow released to what one assumed to be a tiger does not stop after seeing a cow.

In the same way, past actions bear fruit even after obtaining wisdom and knowledge. — 54.

Comment:

The verses 53 and 54 tell that even after enlightenment, consequences of past actions do not vanish. Such is that state of *dharma*. The faulty knowledge of consequences disappears, but one is not free from pain and pleasure brought upon by the past deeds.

**

अजरोऽस्म्यमरोऽस्मीति य आत्मानं प्रपद्यते ।
तदात्मना तिष्ठतोऽस्य कुतः प्रारब्धकल्पना ॥ ५५ ॥

Translation:

"I am eternal, and I am disease free. The soul is the supreme position."

Rooted in the soul thus, where is the imagination of consequence? — 55.

***

प्रारब्धं सिद्ध्यति तदा यदा देहात्मना स्थितिः ।
देहात्मभावो नैवेष्टः प्रारब्धं त्यज्यतामतः ॥ ५६ ॥

Translation:

The consequential actions materialize with the presence of an ego in the body.

As soon as the ego disappears, the consequences do, too. — 56.

***

प्रारब्धकल्पनाप्यस्य देहस्य भ्रान्तिरेव हि ॥ ५७ ॥

Translation:

Only the illusion of the body creates the concept of the consequences. — 57.

***

अध्यस्तस्य कुतस्तत्त्वमसत्यस्य कुतो जनिः ।

अजातस्य कुतो नाशः प्रारब्धमसतः कुतः ॥ ५८ ॥

Translation:

How can an illusion be true and how can something untrue materialize?

How can something that does not materialize end, and how can the consequence's falsehood exist? — 58.

Comment:

Verses 55-58 describe the fallacy of consequences for a yogi. Consequence is a relative term which only exists in two forms: good and bad. If a yogi cuts off their emotions and desires towards the body, the concept of good and bad disappears. Without these comparisons, consequences become void and neutral.

A being's ego isolates the events happening to them from events happening elsewhere. When an entire mountain erodes and becomes sand on a beach, we do not give a second thought about it. However, a zit on our cheeks makes us think about the oily food we had eaten, or the pollution we endure. A promotion at the workplace reminds us of years of our hard work. Thus, actions and consequences exist only along the ego.

Since the supreme soul is immortal and disease free; actions and consequences mean the same to it. The soul is the only actor and exists alone. How can things happen to it if no one else acts? Knowing thus, we realize consequences exist only until we live in the illusion of diversity.

The verse-58 highlights the fact that illusions do not take birth and neither die. Like dreams vanish as soon as the person wakes up, the untrue concepts of actions and consequences vanish once a person attains *samadhi*.

Further, if consequences were never true, and they never materialize, how can someone destroy them? They are a figment of our imagination and become as real as we sink into the sea of illusion. A wise yogi who has realized that the body is an illusion will not care about the consequences, since consequences only affect the body and not the soul.

***

ज्ञानेनाज्ञानकार्यस्य समूलस्य लयो यदि ।
तिष्ठत्ययं कथं देह इति शङ्कावतो जडान् ॥ ५९ ॥

Translation:

If all ignorant actions dissolve into the knowledge.

Where is the possibility of a body then? Only fools doubt this principle. — 59.

***

समाधातुं बाह्यदृष्टच्या प्रारब्धं वदति श्रुतिः ।
न तु देहादिसत्यत्वबोधनाय विपश्चिताम् ॥ ६० ॥

Translation:

The Vedas teach the concept of consequences (virtues and sins) only to make the people who look outward understand.

They do not talk about it for the learned people or for teaching the truth about the body, etc. — 60.

Comment:

The verses 59 and 60 elaborate on the paradox created by earlier verses. On one hand, in verse-54, the Upanishad says, "An arrow released to what one assumed to be a tiger does not stop after seeing a cow. In the same way, past actions bear fruit even after obtaining wisdom and knowledge." In contradiction, the verse-37 says, "In the unending universe, millions of actions assemble. However, with *samadhi*, those actions vanish, and *dharma* multiplies."

Both statements are correct, but for different people. People who practice religion for

~ 58 ~

absolving sins and earning virtues are not free of materialism. By the universal law, their deeds indeed earn virtues and sins. However, they live in the illusion. They perform rituals, read the scriptures, and pray to God. They think they can absolve the accumulated actions with new actions. The Upanishad clarifies that with no methods can one change their past. Present actions alter the future, but everyone must reap what they have already sown.

However, virtues and sins are material and exist only within this temporary universe. A yogi learns to eradicate their desires and emotions together with their ego. If a person has ascended above all material things, the events happening to their bodies do not affect their mental state, intellect, or will. In such a state, it will be true to say that all past and future actions and consequences vanish with liberation.

***

परिपूर्णमनाद्यन्तमप्रमेयमविक्रियम् ।
सद्घनं चिद्घनं नित्यमानन्दघनमव्ययम् ॥ ६१ ॥

Translation:

The universal soul is complete, without beginning and end, imperceptible and inactive.

The treasure of truth, consciousness, continuity, bliss, it is inexhaustible. — 61.

Comment:

This verse describes the soul's properties. 'Complete' means which lacks nothing. The soul has everything possible and everything impossible for the universe.

End and beginning are factors of time, but the soul lives beyond time. It had existed before the universe began and will exist after the collapse.

Imperceptible by senses, intellect, or imagination, it is always present as the soul inside matter. One does not fathom it with the orthodox methods of knowledge. Its knowledge is present in everyone, one only needs to end their illusions.

'Inactive' points to the soul's singular state. Any activity affects others and other activities affect the former. Although the soul lives in the material universe, it does not saturate in its impurities. It stays like a lotus leaf (hydrophobic to the material properties).

A thought experiment in science argues that as soon as activity will stop in an object (the temperature drops to zero Kelvin), it will instantly isolate from the universe. The time ceases for such an inactive object. Thus, the object will vanish never to be seen again. We can assume the same state of the supreme soul, except space and time originate from it. Hence, it acts as the plate that supports the space-time, but exists beyond it.

**

प्रत्यगेकरसं पूर्णमनन्तं सर्वतोमुखम् ।
अहेयमनुपादेयमनाधेयमनाश्रयम् ॥ ६२ ॥

Translation:

The universal soul is resolute, uniform, wholesome, endless, and omnipresent.

It is non-increasing, non-decreasing, self-existent, and self-dependent. — 62.

Comment:

'Resolute' means 'fixed' or 'established'. The soul is not volatile and never leaves.

'Uniform' points to its propertyless-ness. Equivalent everywhere, it has no properties and all properties, all at once.

'Wholesome' means it is one and undivided.

'Endless' means it exists within the boundaries of the universe and beyond. Its expanse is incomprehensible by mind or mathematics.

'Omnipresent' means it is present in every quantum of the universe.

'Non-increasing' and 'non-decreasing' means it is present equally everywhere and does not diminish or dominate with change in place or time.

'Self-existent' means it does not need organs, energy, or another soul to exist.

'Self-dependent' means it does not need dependence on another being for its actions.

***

निर्गुणं निष्क्रियं सूक्ष्मं निर्विकल्पं निरञ्जनम् ।
अनिरूप्यस्वरूपं यन्मनोवाचामगोचरम् ॥ ६३ ॥

Translation:

The universal soul is propertyless, inactive, microscopic, unfragmented, and malice-free.

It is inexplicable and inconceivable by mind and speech. — 63.

Comment:

'Propertyless' means in its original form, the soul is pure and has no properties.

'Inactive' means it does not perform any actions. The universe and its activities are an illusion of the consciousness. Without an ego, the soul is inactive.

'Microscopic' means senses and instruments cannot see it.

'Unfragmented' means diversity is not present in it. It does not show variety and has no choices or options in its existence.

'Malice-free' means the illusions, deeds, virtues, sins, properties, elements, and actions do not affect it. The byproducts of the illusionary universe are a fake dream and do not exist in the soul's pure state.

'Inexplicable' means no one can describe its form with any language.

'Inconceivable' means none of the senses can imagine its form.

***

सत्समृद्धं स्वतःसिद्धं शुद्धं बुद्धमनीदृशम् ।
एकमेवाद्वयं ब्रह्म नेह नानास्ति किंचन ॥ ६४ ॥

Translation:

The universal soul exists full of truth and is of self-form, is pure, wise, and incomparable.

It is the alpha and the beta. Nothing else exists. — 64.

Comment:

The universal spirit is the complete truth. It is real in its entirety and illusion has no place in it.

It exists in its own form. Independent and self-existent, it does not need another factor.

'Pure' means it is free of impurities of the material universe.

'Wise' means it holds the universe's knowledge and beyond. It exists as pure knowledge (spiritual), free of any material and malice.

'Incomparable' means no picture or imagination can produce its image. None of the material or spiritual objects imagined by the consciousness can compare to it.

'Alpha' and 'beta' point to the god and the spirit (soul in the material beings). The verse says that the discrimination between God and soul does not exist. Only the supreme, universal soul is the truth in the material and the spiritual.

***

स्वानुभूत्या स्वयं ज्ञात्वा स्वमात्मानमखण्डितम् ।
स सिद्धः सुसुखं तिष्ठन् निर्विकल्पात्मनात्मनि ॥ ६५ ॥

Translation:

From your experiences, know your own soul as singular.

Thus, sit in resolution and bliss within your one and only soul. — 65.

Comment:

The sage asks his student to inspect with their own intellect and find the universal soul in themselves. Since the universal soul is already present in everyone, searching for it elsewhere makes no sense. A person knows themselves up-close and the best. So, why search the God at other places?

Once one finds the ultimate knowledge, they become the image of the soul—resolute and blissful.

***

क्व गतं केन वा नीतं कुत्र लीनमिदं जगत् ।
अधुनैव मया दृष्टं नास्ति किं महदद्भुतम् ॥ ६६ ॥

Translation:

Where did the world go, and who removed it? Where did it disappear?

I could see it a moment ago. Does it not exist now? Huge surprise! — 66.

Comment:

The teacher's grace enlightened the student. They saw themselves under a new light. They wondered about the illusion that was present a moment ago. That illusion was real until they had found the true reality. They are amazed at how something has vanished without a trace.

***

किं हेयं किमुपादेयं किमन्यत्किंविलक्षणम् ।
अखण्डानन्दपीयूषपूर्णब्रह्ममहार्णवे ॥ ६७ ॥

Translation:

What is there to gain? What is there to lose? Is there even anything else? Is anything stranger?

This is the unfragmented sea of ambrosia that is the universe. — 67.

***

न किंचिदत्र पश्यामि न शृणोमि न वेद्म्यहम् ।
स्वात्मनैव सदानन्दरूपेणास्मि स्वलक्षणः ॥ ६८ ॥

Translation:

Here I do not see, hear, or know anything.

I am set up in my own blissful soul, with my own properties. — 68.

असङ्गोऽहमनङ्गोऽहमलिङ्गोऽहमहं हरिः ।
प्रशान्तोऽहमनन्तोऽहं परिपूर्णश्चिरन्तनः ॥ ६९ ॥

Translation:

I am company free, organ free, sign free, and self-righteous god.

I am ever-calm, unending, complete, and ancestor of the most ancient. — 69.

अकर्ताहमभोक्ताहमविकारोऽहमव्ययः ।
शुद्धो बोधस्वरूपोऽहं केवलोऽहं सदाशिवः ॥ ७० ॥

Translation:

I am a non-actor, non-consumer, non-doped, and invariable.

I am pure wisdom and the only ever *Shiva*. — 70

Comment:

In verses 67-70, the student realizes the unity and the singularity of the soul.

***

एतां विद्यामपान्तरतमाय ददौ ।
अपान्तरतमो ब्रह्मणे ददौ ।
ब्रह्मा घोराङ्गिरसे ददौ ।

घोराङ्गिरा रैक्वाय ददौ ।
रैक्वो रामाय ददौ ।
रामः सर्वेभ्यो भूतेभ्यो ददावित्येतन्निर्वाणानुशासनं
वेदानुशासनं वेदानुशासनमित्युपनिषत् ॥ ७१ ॥

Translation:

Shiva gave this knowledge to Apantaratam.

Apantaratam gave it to Brahma.

Brahma gave it to Angiras.

Angiras gave it to Raikva.

Raikva gave it to Parashuram.

Parashuram presented it to all beings. It is the order for liberation. This is the Veda's order. This is the Veda's order. The Upanishad is complete. — 71.

Comment:

This verse dictates the chronology of this knowledge. The sages have divided the Hindu scriptures into two parts: *shruti* 'heard' and *smriti* 'memory'. *Smriti* are the texts which the sages wrote from memory of events. They are less credible, as they have a probability of being corrupt. One cannot trust memory as it can be faulty, no matter how wise and intelligent the person is. The *Puranas* 'ancient history' and the *Itihasas* 'history' are its examples. The other scriptures are *shruti*, which pass down generations of people by telling and retelling the exact verses. They have their origin in the supreme God. Vedas and Upanishads are the examples of *shruti*.

The *Adhyatma Upanishad* comes from the mouth of the supreme God *Shiva*. He taught it to his student, *Apantaratam*. *Apantaratam* 'without internal darkness' is the first incarnation of the sage who organizes the Vedas from time to time.

Upon praying to *Vishnu*, *Brahma* learned the eternal knowledge. He uttered the same in one alphabet to sage *Narad*, who divided it into four parts and gave it to the sages. Sage *Ved-Vyas* 'creator of the Vedas' organizes the verses to complete the knowledge in each age. In each age, the scriptures exchanges hands and break down in several parts. *Ved-Vyas* is a position held by the incarnations of *Apantaratam*. The incarnation in our age is the sage *Krishna-Dwaipayan*.

Apantaratam gave this knowledge to the creator of the world, *Brahma*. *Brahma* gave it to the sage *Angiras*. *Angiras* is *Brahma's* son and later god *Agni* 'fire' adopted him. He is one of the *prajapatis* 'creators of life' and is the seer of many verses in the Vedas. With his austere powers, he became brighter than the fire. *Agni*, diminished by his powers, requested him to take his position.

He did not want to insult the standing god. He asked *Agni* to adopt him. Only then, he took the position as an inheritance. Hence, *Angiras* is the present god of fire.

Angiras gave the knowledge to sage *Raikva* (one of the revered sages). *Raikva* gave it to sage *Parashuram* (the 16th avatar of *Vishnu* out of the twenty-two avatars). *Parashuram* presented this knowledge for the welfare of the world to his students.

This Upanishad extracts the essence from the Vedas. If Vedas teach about the rituals, Adhyatma Upanishad teaches the symbolism behind those rituals. It presents the practical path a yogi can take to reach liberation. This is the secretive knowledge the sages have given for the welfare of the soulful, spiritually inclined people.

The Prayer for Peace

॥शांतिपाठः ॥

ॐ पूर्णमदः पूर्णमिदं पूर्णात्पूर्णमुदच्यते ।

पूर्णस्य पूर्णमादाय पूर्णमेवावशिष्यते ॥

ॐ शान्तिः शान्तिः शान्तिः ॥

Translation:

Om is whole in the beginning and is whole here. The wholesome of this universe takes birth from that singularity.

Remove this universe from that singularity, and the remaining is still whole.

Om! Peace! Peace! Peace!

॥इत्यध्यात्मोपनिषत्समाप्ता ॥

Translation:

This is the end of Adhyatma Upanishad.

About Author

An expert on Hindu mythology, Digvijay's passion for spiritual writing was inspired by the wisdom in ancient Indian literature. On his blog, he writes about meditation, yoga, and personal transformation.

He has 6+ years of experience in web content writing and copywriting, and 3+ years of experience in sales and marketing. His first book, 'Gurukul Tales–Teacher Student Stories from Ancient India' ranked #2 on Amazon in 'Mythology and Folk tales' and #3 in 'Children's Short Stories'.

With his family, he lives in Bengaluru, India. His favorite pastime is messing about with his son. Except books, he is a fan of music, irrespective of its genre, and likes mind-melting movies.